Georg Trakl

by

MAIRE JAANUS KURRIK

 *Columbia University Press*

NEW YORK & LONDON 1974

COLUMBIA ESSAYS ON MODERN WRITERS
is a series of critical studies of English,
Continental, and other writers whose works are of contemporary
artistic and intellectual significance.

Editor

George Stade

Advisory Editors

Jacques Barzun   W. T. H. Jackson   Joseph A. Mazzeo

Georg Trakl is Number 72 of the series

MAIRE JAANUS KURRIK
is Assistant Professor of English at Barnard College.

Acknowledgment is made to Otto Müller Verlag,
Salzburg, for permission to quote from Georg
Trakl's *Dichtungen und Briefe,* published in 1969,
and to Farrar, Straus & Giroux, Inc., for permission
to quote four lines from John Berryman's
Delusions, etc., published in 1972.

Library of Congress Cataloging in Publication Data

Kurrik, Maire Jaanus.
 Georg Trakl.
 (Columbia essays on modern writers, no. 72)
 1. Trakl, Georg, 1887–1914—Criticism and interpretation.   I. Series.
 PT2642.R22Z69   831'.9'12   74-1106
 ISBN 0-231-03501-2

Copyright © 1974 Columbia University Press
Printed in the United States of America

Georg Trakl

Georg Trakl's life is the coincidence of mental disease and art. Trakl died of an overdose of cocaine in a mental hospital in Cracow in 1914, at the age of twenty-seven. In an official letter his condition was defined as dementia praecox or schizophrenia. The accuracy of the diagnosis is something we may doubt; that he suffered from a psychosis of some sort is indubitable. The majority of the studies on Trakl ignore the fact of his disease and its possible influence on his poetry. Because his poetry, undeniably, has aesthetic quality and because it attests to a formal development, the assumption has been that it must be intelligible, or if not that, then mystically inspired or prophetic. Only Emil Staiger and Wolfgang Schneditz have dared to link his unintelligibility to his derangement. And rightly so. For Trakl's poetry leads us ultimately to the interiority that lies behind language, to naked primary process where there is no longer any directing idea to control the play of involuntary pathological associations and complexes. Trakl's art challenges us to dissociate order and meaning, and to discriminate between them in a new way.

We uphold the notion of art as something created by the whole psyche, by the conscious and the unconscious. We accept that a temporary regression from the world of rational consciousness may be a necessary moment in poetic creation, but we stress conscious ego control no matter how much unconscious material an artist absorbs or how much use he makes of the primary process, that is, the processes operating in the id, to structure his creations. Yet, Trakl's case suggests that the aesthetic intention is, indeed, as Husserl would argue and as our rare, phenomenally beautiful dreams confirm, anterior to consciousness or to mental disease—an intentionality given with the human psyche. It suggests that the critical issue should not be the overly much feared one of reducing genius to pathology, but the more humane one of granting pathology a measure of genius. It means allowing that a schizophrenic *poem*, though the very idea of it may seem incongruous and paradoxical, is possible. It also means realizing that even disease evinces a form and a development, and that artistic development may not be only the consequence of intact ego functions. To force Trakl to be intelligible is exactly to ignore the challenges posed by the conjunction of art and disease: the challenge to accept the idea that creative cognition functions with and on all levels of the psyche, the challenge to break the customary association of creativity and consciousness, and the challenge to share what are in essence so radically altered and alien states of consciousness that the ordinary critic can have had no experience of them.

Trakl's mature verse, written between 1909 and 1914, fills one not very thick volume. To this the elaborate 1969 historical-critical edition of his works adds 145 short letters. We know very little about Trakl and much of the information comes from the reminiscences of friends who remained overly impressed by his strange utterances and behavior and his genuine desperation. At least one of these acquaintances, Rudolf Kassner, more distant and less awed by Trakl, commented that there was something schizophrenic about him which can be felt in his poetry as well. We learn that he struck everyone as solitary and inaccessible, that he was unusually quiet, and that when he did speak it was in the oracular, enigmatic manner of his poetry, with a thundering, but estranged voice. His conversation was always a monologue, his eyes fixed on something distant. To one friend he said that he never saw people at all and had no notion of their physiognomy. To another he said that until the age of twenty he noticed nothing in his environment except the water. We hear of his attempts to drown himself at the age of eight by walking into a pond, of his drug and alcohol addiction beginning at the age of fifteen, and of his early failure in school. Later both the reports and the letters attest to constant depressions, to severe anxiety attacks, to his fears of being followed and persecuted, and to his fantasies of punishment. In the light of this and other information it is likely that the overdose of cocaine in Cracow was intentional.

In World War I Trakl was left to care for over ninety fatally wounded men in a barn without the drugs necessary to relieve them in any way. He was by training only a pharmacist. Outside the barn he could see the bodies of suspected enemy sympathizers hanging from trees. Inside Trakl witnessed the suicide of one of the wounded. Not too long after this episode Trakl attempted to shoot himself, but was held back and sent to Cracow for mental observation. If—and it is a large if—Trakl had any chance of surviving, despite his psychosis and his self-destructive and addictive impulses, he had none in a world where traumatic experiences such as the above were possible. The terrible, final episode of Trakl's life is commemorated by the late John Berryman in "Drugs Alcohol Little Sister" and made exemplary in a manner that would have been alien to the frightened young man in Cracow, who both feared and desired death, and who may have killed himself because he suffered from the delusion that he was to be condemned to death in a military court for his failure on the battlefield.

> for let us not all together in such pain
> dumb apart pale into oblivion—no!
> Trakl, con the male nurse.
> Surmounted by carrion, cry out   and overdose & go.

From the scant details of Trakl's life the eminent Jungian psychologist, Erich Neumann, has pieced together a psychic biography. Neumann postulates that, as with every neurosis,

Trakl's bears witness to a failure in the primary emotional relationships, in Trakl's case the relationship to his mother and sister. Trakl's mother was very likely herself an addict; she was distant from her family, withdrawn from them for days, remote, cold, and interested primarily in her antiques. Neumann connects Trakl's earliest as well as subsequent academic and social failures and his adolescent rebelliousness to the original loss of his mother's love.

Trakl's second attempt at a close human relationship, with his younger sister, Grete, also came to grief. Grete, Trakl's junior by five years, was musically gifted, passionate, erratic, wild, and also addicted to drugs; she shot herself in 1917. She was for Trakl in his youth "the most beautiful girl, the greatest artist, the most extraordinary woman," and throughout his life, according to one report, Trakl surrounded her with "tender and angry care." In childhood, Neumann speculates, the brother and sister lived in a state of symbiotic closeness; at puberty their union was ruptured by the act of incest. (The *de facto* nature of the incest has been accepted by all but a few commentators; amongst Trakl's friends only Erhard Buschbeck, who it seems was also briefly Grete's lover, expressly denied it. In 1954 Theodor Spoerri claimed to have positive proof for the occurrence which, however, he claimed not to be able to divulge out of consideration for the living members of the family.) The symbiotic nature of the primary relationship led Trakl, according to Neumann, to experience the incest as a murderous and sinful deed, in fact, as the primordial fall and destruction of what Trakl called the "blue" paradise of innocence, in which there is no sexual gender and we possess the androgynous nature of the primitive mythic man. In the poem "Passion," written in 1914, we read:

> And following the sister's shadow;
> Dark love
> Of a wild race . . . .

> Under dark firs
> Two wolves mingled their blood
> In a stony embrace; as gold
> The cloud lost itself over the footpath,
> Patience and silence of childhood.

The sexual violence committed upon the sister transformed him as brother into a murderous criminal and cripple and into the destroyer in himself of the innocent youth that he was. In "Dream and Madness" he confesses:

> Hate burned away his heart, lust, when, in the greening summer garden, he violated the silent child, recognizing in the radiant one his own benighted face.

Neumann uses the adolescent episode to explain the later experiences of terror, guilt, and depersonalization, as well as his notorious ambivalence. Neumann's approach does not account for how this ambivalence reached such immense proportions, how it reached into the innermost meaning of single words to brand them with an open instability; nor does it account for the intensification of Trakl's guilt to the point where he suffers from delusions of punishment. Any genetic approach encourages us to see Trakl's work in the light of a repetition compulsion: there was the painful and traumatic experience, and the purpose of the repetition here—as in dreams or tragedy—is to achieve mastery over that experience. Trakl's curiously limited vocabularly and imagery and his obsessive repetitiousness would in fact encourage such a view, but a genetic approach would still not account for the dynamic transformation of his images and the equally dynamic changes in his style and technique.

For Neumann the crisis in puberty is the definitive one in Trakl's life which shattered his chances for full individuation and maturation. In order to make, if not his aesthetic development, at least the sheer mystery of his creative achievment somehow intelligible, Neumann has recourse to the Jungian scheme of the psyche. Since the anima mediates between the collective unconscious and the personal unconscious in Jung's vision, Neumann argues that the more estranged Trakl became from the world of rational consciousness in his intense search for and relationship to his sister, the more intimate he was with the world of the collective unconscious where the anima archetypes reign. He compensated for the lost chance of developing a fully integrated self by the development of what Neumann calls a "mythic ego." He became a "transpersonal, archaic singer." However, the mythological and primordial imagery in Trakl's poetry is merely fragmentary. And there is no coherent private myth of the kind that Blake, for example, created. There is also no coherent symbolism, only a limited number of suggestive, ambivalent, and incomplete symbols, autistically intertwined. Trakl was too far removed from all that is conscious and rational to create either. The creation of a coherent myth is always in part a conscious, an intellectual, achievement, and its purpose, according to Lévi-Straus, is "to provide a logical model capable of overcoming contradictions." Authentic symbols are, for Jung, signs of an integration of consciousness and the unconscious; they fuse opposition in a convincing "aesthetic form" which is "indissoluble" and "unassailable." Trakl's symbols are inherently antithetical; worse still, they break down and are distorted in a chaotic randomness.

Earlier critics of Trakl, including Heidegger, tended to ignore both the problem of his development and his style in favor of reconstructing his over-all world vision. This vision was literally "created" by extracting single images from various poems and reordering them under a guiding idea or theme invented by the critic. More recently, critics have divided his brief creative span into three major phases by paying particular attention to stylistic changes. But the work in this area has not been speculative; it has either been purely descriptive or it has sought to explain technical advances in terms of formal influences by other poets. But just as only those unconscious materials which can be adapted to the reality of formal structures pass into language, so new forms or new formal influences and their application only become possible at certain psychic stages. The causal source studies on Trakl forget that these "influences" do not initiate but only meet and feed his development. To explain Trakl's development and maturation in language—and it is the only maturation and triumph that his otherwise pathetic life presents—we must postulate a particularly intense relationship to language: in a sense, what one could call a transference to language itself. For dreams and disease are two ways into the unconscious, but language is a third. It is language, not disease, that made his art, but it is also language foremost that was affected by the progress of his disease.

Trakl's work starts out from silence. Every critic has been struck by Trakl's intimacy with silence and emptiness. Rilke noted it when he said of "Helian" that "it is built on its pauses, a few satisfactions about the limitless wordless: so stand the lines. Like fences in a flat land beyond which extends the unfenced in an unpossessable vastness." The void surrounding Trakl's words is the crucial dimension of his verse out of which things emerge as in the voided state of consciousness in sleep. Trakl's poetry presents the phenomenon of a transference to language, provoked by his existence in the void. He did not experience language as an objective given that can be used and molded, but as the shape of his true inner inexpressible self. From the first, all the words that did not express his inner being were abolished. They were less authentic than silence. However, silence was also terrifying, as terrifying in fact as it can only be when language is invested with all of reality and identified with self. Thus when we see Trakl lost during the task of composition in antitheses and meaningless confusion, or see him experience a projection of himself, lost and exiled in his own mental landscape, we also feel that Rilke's awesome query, "Who could he have been?" was never answered by Trakl himself and may never be answered until we know much more about the psychological interpretation of syntactic structures than we do now.

Even the juvenilia, Trakl's earliest, rather unoriginal, and aesthetically valueless poems, prose, and drama-fragments, published by Buschbeck in 1939 (but rightly rejected by Trakl himself from inclusion in the collection of his poems in preparation during his lifetime), are interesting in what they reveal about his attitude to language. At this point Trakl experiments with a variety of verse forms and borrows heavily — but the very restlessness of the adolescent imitations and experimentations serves to point to his discontent with the poetic language that he inherits. The discontent emerges more clearly in the poetry itself as a continual lament and complaint about language as impotent, sterile, and incapable of incarnating experience or the self.

The poetic language that he inherits seems to Trakl a too conscious and reflective kind of language, a language that pushes one into making reflected, summarizing statements about existence. What strikes Trakl as significant, though undefinable, about his experience is his special moods of revery and dream. Words are like mere masks compared to the something else that is vaguely felt within. Also, the surface impressions that we receive from the outer world are not the point; thus it is characteristic of these early verses to suggest that beneath the surface impression of things there are other, more mysterious things that emerge: ominous or ineffable mysteries, artificial paradises or grotesque visions, unusual melodies, or most frequently, an incomprehensible, but as if embodied, silence. Interestingly, Trakl also feels such a disjunction between the surface and the underlying reality in himself; in a poem, "The Horror," he watches himself in a state of dissociation in which he cannot make his own mirror image the object of his reflection; the image in the mirror with which he is left alone is that of himself as a murderer. Similarly, in "Nature-theater" he sees himself as an innocent child, but the vision strikes him with the unreality of a stage spectacle; it makes him cry, but it is "distant from his comprehension." Inner and outer reality are split; both appear ghostly, incomprehensible, absurd, and distant. Poems are "substanceless," "vain," and "inglorious." Therefore, the conscious world with its impressions and states of reflection is rejected, and together with this goes a disillusionment with language. More valid for Trakl than the linguistic sphere are the verbally less easily definable semiconscious states of feeling, revery, intuition, and dream, and the voice of the sexual instincts.

In a review of a neo-romantic drama written in 1908, Trakl praises the language that has the power to evoke such moods and attributes this power particularly to the melodic aspect of language:

It is extraordinary how these verses penetrate the problem, how often the sound of the word expresses an unutterable thought and holds fast the fleeting mood. In these lines there is something of the sweet, feminine rhetoric which seduces us to listen to the melos of the word and ignore its content and significance; the minor key of this language puts the sensibilities into a mediative mood and fills the blood with dreamy fatigue.

The praise expresses Trakl's own ideal at this time. He separates the word considered as sound or melody from the word considered as the expression of an idea or as meaning. Audible harmony or music is a compromise between language and silence. If we can say, following de Saussure, that the phonetic aspect of language is its more unconscious aspect and grammar its conscious aspect, we can speculate that Trakl's intense relationship to language began with an immediate attraction to what was, on the surface, more unconscious about it, its sound value and melody. He identified his true inner self with the ineffable, with melody.

In Trakl's first major phase as a poet acoustical activity predominates. From 1909 to 1912 he composed almost exclusively in rhymed quatrains and sonnets. Rhythm and rhyme, Max Rieser has argued, reduce affective pressure. They have the ability to allay strong feelings and to limit their intensity. Rhyme is a superstructure that augments the effect of rhythm; and rhythm is repetition, an acoustical form of associational activity. On the one hand, rhythm and rhyme are, as a way of composing, a very strict form of mental activity and demanding of self-discipline. As such they suited Trakl, who could still write with some confidence in 1909 that "to fasten and clarify" his "ceaselessly changing and doubting nature. . . . is the main thing that [he has] ever hoped for." On the other hand, they are for Trakl, clearly, an escape into what is containing and protective, soothing and lulling, druglike and semiconscious; even more, they are an attempt at repression, a rejection of an aspect of reality. A letter written in 1908 confirms this:

> I believe it would be terrible to live ever so: in full consciousness of all the animalistic instincts that propel life through the ages. I have experienced, smelled, touched the most frightening possibilities within myself, have heard the demons howling in my blood. . . . What a horrible nightmare!
> Gone! Today this vision of reality has again sunk into nothingness, distant from me are the things, more distant still their voice, and I again listen, all animated ear, to the melodies which are in me, and my winged eye again dreams its images, which are more beautiful than all reality! I am one again, am my world! My whole, beautiful world, filled with unending euphony.

The letter acknowleges that melody is a way of shutting out the voices of instinctual life Trakl hears "howling in his blood," and which he evidently cannot deal with. The split in language parallels a split in the self between "dream" and "nightmare." It allows Trakl to idealize the "dream" and to reject the "nightmare" by distancing and distortion. However, a repressed idea may reappear, according to Freud, "in the guise of a particular qualitative tone," or it may be "transformed to anxiety." Initially, Trakl's repression appears to be successful.

A number of these poems are harmonious, positively toned, and superficially they can be read as mood lyrics or romantic ballads, for example, "The Beautiful City" and "The Young Maid." Read glancingly they need not strike one as being particularly personal. But in the light of Trakl's own confession, a poem such as "The Rats" is clearly an example of the instinctual life returning in a derivative and distanced form. Also the tone of melancholy which insinuates itself even into the most harmonious and positive poems is too marked and persistent not to be noticed—and to be noticed especially as something that somehow always misses its object or is beyond it or in excess of it—a seemingly separate, objectless affect. Finally, in the latter half of this period a kind of anxiety about the ghostly, incomprehensible nature of a gyrating, unreal, or often senselessly repulsive or threatening reality seems to develop. And such anxiety is a sign that the repression is failing. This cycle of repression, its failure, and the return of the repressed in the form of anxiety or dread comes to be a fundamental one in Trakl's work.

Trakl's attempt to musicalize his experience—to work with rhythm and rhyme, acoustical association and repetition, and the syllable, the primary building element of the lyric, rather than with language as a signifier of meanings and relationships—had further consequences. It sealed his alienation from the outer world and from language, as we know it, as a causal, connective structure concerned with relationships. Gradually and subtly, the initial withdrawal from an aspect of reality and an aspect of language lead to a complete loss of reality in Trakl. Rhythm and rhyme, by providing Trakl with a semblance of coherence, actually allowed more of the disorder and incoherence that he experienced to pass into his verse. For rhymed harmony can disguise chaos, even while secretly encouraging it with its regularity and uniformity, its semblance of synthesis and unity. Furthermore, because the semblance of order comes into being as the consequence of a rather free or free-associational treatment of an area of language, of its sound aspect, the habit of free-association passes gradually to other aspects of language.

Trakl's discourse in these poems becomes increasingly acausal and discontinuous. At first every other line, then each line in the poems comes to lose its connection to what precedes it. The lines or images stand isolated or their mysterious connection depends upon some inner complex of associations or affects that are difficult to ferret out. In a letter of 1910 Trakl called this his "imagist manner" which entailed a "welding together" of heterogeneous images and which must create the impression of "a living fever" to be effective. Critics have called the effect that these poems give "kaleidoscopic" or "mosaic-like," and one critic has termed the poems of this phase "carousel-like." Trakl's own term, "a living fever," is perhaps most apt for these discontinuous lines from the poem "Gloom":

> World-woe spirits through the afternoon.
> Huts flee through gardens brown and waste.
>
> On the withered meadow runs a child
> And plays with its eyes black and smooth.
> Gold drips from the bushes sad and weak.
> An old man turns himself sadly in the wind.

Even in the rhymed German version of the poem, written at the end of 1912 and thus at the end of Trakl's rhymed period, the rhyme no longer serves to harmonize or to unify. A feverish anxiety and melancholy that exceed the individual images are what characterize and unify this poem. Hereafter the overthrow of a rhyme that has become merely gratuitous follows as a matter of course.

"Soul of Life," a rhymed poem written approximately in the middle of this first period, shows in a particularly discordant form some of the tensions and contradictory ways of representation that characterize this period.

> Verfall, der weich das Laub umdüstert,
> Es wohnt im Wald sein weites Schweigen.
> Bald scheint ein Dorf sich geisterhaft zu neigen.
> Der Schwester Mund in schwarzen Zweigen flüstert.
>
> Der Einsame wird bald entgleiten,
> Vielleicht ein Hirt auf dunklen Pfaden.
> Ein Tier tritt leise aus den Baumarkaden,
> Indes die Lider sich vor Gottheit weiten.
>
> Der blaue Fluss rinnt schön hinunter,
> Gewölke sich am Abend zeigen;
> Die Seele auch in engelhaftem Schweigen.
> Vergängliche Gebilde gehen unter.
>
> (Decay, which softly glooms around the leaves,
> In the forest lives its wide silence.
> Soon a hamlet seems spectrally to bow itself.
> The sister's mouth whispers in black branches.
>
> The lonely one will soon escape,
> Perhaps a shepherd on dark paths.
> An animal steps silently out of the trees' arcades,
> As the eyelids widen themselves before divinity.
>
> The blue stream runs lovely down
> Clouds show themselves at evening;
> The soul also in angel-like silence.
> Transient images are perishing.)

In the poem we seem to hear two different kinds of discourse. The last stanza is metrically even, smooth, and melodious. It

[15]

is wholly Trakl's world of beautiful melos where we are removed from actuality and its pressures. The "soul" is in a state of "angellike silence" because the flow of the song transforms and cancels the flow of decay. Harmony distances and disguises; it turns the decay into a spectacle which is perceived as the transience of a flowing sound. Nature still appears in this last stanza as a mirror and reservoir of analogies for subjective perceptions; "stream" and "cloud" are conventional images of transience.

The discourse in the first two stanzas is the acausal, discontinuous, somewhat mysterious, and eerie discourse that we encountered in "Gloom." Here as there, what matters is the lack not only of obvious connections between lines and images but also of clear distinctions between nature and man, animate and inanimate, mobile and immobile, inside and outside, subject and object. "Huts flee," "a hamlet" seems "to bow itself," and a child "plays" with its eyes. We have regressed to the undifferentiated world of primitive mentality where the fundamental distinction between objective and subjective reality is dissolved. How is "the lonely one" or the "sister's mouth" connected to natural decay or its main attribute, silence, or to the pastoral realm of shepherds and divinity? How is "an animal" connected to all these, and why does it step forth just "as the eyelids widen themselves before divinity"? We are not in the presence of an ensouled landscape where subject and object interpenetrate each other or stand for each other, but have merely the suggestive remnant of such a process. We are rather in the world of dreams where transitions, events, and things simply occur, or appear, or are in their own reality. It is a world of irrational conjunctions where configurational perceptions are registered merely by contiguity.

Nature, though present fragmentarily in the poem, ceases to matter as an objective outer reality; its sinking decay is transformed in a soft circling motion, into a "wide silence." The circular motion acts as a kind of intersection between the vertical sinking motion of decay and decline and the horizontal motion usually associated in Trakl with expansion, sound or silence, and arrested time. For just as the "silence" is about to be complete because all of reality ("the hamlet") is sinking away, the silence is interrupted by the "whispers" of the sister. But this voice already comes from the interior memory. It is an interference, an irruption from the unconscious, caused by some kind of inner conflict, which disturbs the flow of association. The interrupted silence is recovered by a new, but now entirely inner movement toward decline, sinking, the vertical; but whether "the lonely one" succeeds in attaining the expanded state of vision and arrested time is left open. For he may only "perhaps" move as a shepherd, and just "as" the expanded state is to occur, "an animal steps silently out of the trees' arcades." That animal can itself be the vision and as such either a holy or an unholy one. Uncertainty and openness come to be more and more characteristic of Trakl the further he penetrates into his interiority. Repeatedly the fundamental inner, unconscious, but transcendent state for which he will aim—as in the climactic line: "As the eyelids widen themselves before divinity"—will either fail him or remain mysteriously ambivalent and incomplete.

If we study this poem in the context of his other poems from this period, we find that it is merely a new and different constellation of images that have already been constituted. Trakl's reservoir of analogies and imaginative stimulants is not the outer world or perception, but his inner world, his own poetry. For example, the line "The sister's mouth whispers in black branches" is a new and more striking formulation of a basic image of something taking place through trees which occurs in other poems: in "Decay," the line "The blackbird laments in the defoliated branches"; in "Bright Spring," "A waxen face flows through alders" and "O mouth that trembles through the white willow"; in "All Souls," "The sighing of lovers breathes in branches." Trakl's excessive dependence on self-repetition suggests a withdrawal into the self where the search continues for another reality, differently constituted, which would allow him to escape both the pressures of outer reality and those that arise from within.

The fact of Trakl's repetitiousness is reinforced when we look at his drafts; they reveal that he never permanently abandoned anything that he had composed. For example, Walther Killy's study of the "Helian-complex," the various drafts of the poem, shows that the complex also yielded "Evening Song," "To the Sister," and "Decline." The verbal economy suggests that Trakl had few words and that he cherished them with desperation, for the fearful alternative was an exile to muteness and silence. Killy's study also proves that Trakl's manner of composition was not guided by any definite intuitions about its end, form, or meaning. The drafts give no evidence of a process of prefiguration or of a guiding idea. Trakl composed as he lived, in darkness and incertitude. Striking but incoherent images of affect—such as "His breath drinks icy gold," "The hands stir the age of bluish waters," "Silver, against a bare wall, a child's skeleton smashes," "O the blood that runs from the throat of the musical one," "And angels stalk noiselessly out of the blue/ Eyes of lovers," "The blue shape of man would pass through his legend," "The redeeming head moulded of hard metals"—are alogically conjoined in the mature poetry where a great deal of effort seems, however, to have been spent on color and sound patterns, and on patterns of movement. The chaotic genesis and the indeterminable development of a Trakl poem are one reason why the availability of all known variants of a poem, with the appearance of the 1969 historical-critical edition of his works, has not, despite all hopes, made imminent the solution of the problems posed by his works, foremost the problem of their meaning.

The second phase of Trakl's development, which begins late in the year 1912 and which includes all but a handful of poems written in the late spring and summer of 1914 before his death, is the most remarkable and most creative phase of his life; it is the period which makes him, in the words of a *Times Literary Supplement* reviewer, one of "the few giants among modern German-language poets." On the whole, it is a period in which we see the elaboration of an increasingly fantastic substitute reality and its collapse. At first the substitute reality aims to construct an ideal imagined past. Later a violently antithetical fantasy world of good and evil seeks to replace the real world. At the same time Trakl's efforts to conjoin or make coherent his increasingly dissociated self approach a crisis and finally an impasse.

Reading the poems of this and his final phase can make one feel as if Trakl had personally discovered the arbitrary character of linguistic signs, as if Wittgenstein's philosophic insight had been his: that outside of a conventionally established system of signs, words are entirely free and lawless, since they do not look like the things they designate anyway. We are stunned and confused by what appears to be an entirely willful use of language; we are tempted to pass Trakl's poems off as mere play with words together with the numerous critics who have done so, or to question, as was done at a top-level literary conference, whether Trakl's poetry is not *"Kitsch."* Surely it is a paradoxical situation in which the poetry of a declared genius is suspected also of being nonsensical. Is it not possible, then, to suspect that Trakl's seemingly "free" use of language must be brought together with the conditions of his disease and even with the original diagnosis in Cracow?

Trakl did not manage to make a great impact in his time, but already in May, 1912, he had met Ludwig von Ficker, who became his great supporter and admirer, and his poetry began to appear regularly in the latter's influential magazine, *Der Brenner*. In the autumn of 1912, other friends attempted to get a collection of Trakl's verses published. Their effort did not succeed, but in April, 1913, the new Kurt Wolff publishing house inquired after his poetry and published a small selection shortly thereafter. A second publication followed, but Trakl did not live to see it. In many ways Trakl was receiving encouragement and support, but his melancholy and depressions do not seem to have been allayed. Neither success nor art itself had any cathartic effect on Trakl. All in all one feels how accurate Thomas Mann was when he wrote after reading Trakl: "A sad and lonely life has become intensive poetry here, but it is, despite all the ardour of expression, a painful self-enclosed sphere, which is not concerned with 'understanding' in the rational sense of the word." Trakl lived cut off from exchange with others and the outside world, and from the stimulation and change that new sense perceptions, experiences, or relationships might bring. His loss of contact with the world of others and with himself echoes in the word-loneliness of his poetry.

The few curt letters that we have from him indicate increasing "despair." "The last weeks were again a chain of sickness and despair," he writes in February, 1913, and in the same month we are given an alarming self-portrayal, one which seems to suggest that his only alternatives were a melancholy dreaming or a terrifying physical and mental state of deathly petrification: "Strange showers of transformation, experienced bodily to the point where it is unbearable, visions of darkness, culminating in the certitude of having died, trances to the point of stony torpidity; and the further-dreaming of sad dreams." "Nothing remains," he continues in March, 1913, "but a feeling of wild despair and a horror at this chaotic existence." The despair paralyzed him and isolated him. According to Buschbeck: "He avoided restaurants out of fear of the waiter; traveling out of fear of the other travelers." Such anxiety made his various unsuccessful attempts to become economically independent futile from the start. For example, on December 1, 1912, Trakl was to start a post with the Viennese ministry of labor; he obtained a one-month postponement; when he began the job he lasted with it for two hours and sought his dismissal the next day. Thereafter he had no employment except for a period of less than one month, and he was in constant financial difficulty. In 1914 Ficker received 100,000 crowns from an unknown donor (who turned out to be Wittgenstein) to distribute among worthy Austrian poets. Ficker decided immediately to give 20,000 crowns each to Rilke and Trakl, but when they went to the bank to take out a part of it, Trakl was seized by such fear that he ran away bathed in sweat. Though the financial worries are also a constant theme in the letters, they in no way account for these words written in November, 1913: "In my confusion and all the despair of the recent times, I no longer know how I shall still live. I have indeed met people here who are willing to help; but it will appear to me that they cannot help me and it will all end in the dark." What Trakl could not dominate in his inner mental experience—his profound insecurity, despair, anxiety, and his terror of engulfment or petrification—he could also eventually not keep out of his poetry.

Some critics account for the changes in Trakl's discourse by his renewed preoccupation with Rimbaud in the late autumn of 1912 (particularly through K. L. Ammer's influential translation of 1907) and by his adoption, in general, of a Symbolist manner of composing. "Helian" has been called "the first major poem in German written in an uncompromisingly Symbolist style." What does make Trakl's poems similar to the modern Symbolist poem is particularly the manner in which they draw attention to the individual word. In modern Symbolist poetry our attention is focused on the single word, as Roland Barthes says, because the word has ceased to be primarily relational and connective; its functional nature in the whole of a grammatical context is diminished, because the latter has lost its domination. Given the devaluation of grammar, the word emerges and attains a density by itself. It becomes "encyclopaedic" and "reduced to a sort of zero degree, pregnant with all past and future specifications."

Trakl's words, isolated in silence, have both a vertical and a horizontal dimension. By horizontal I mean the inevitable rootedness of language in conventional meanings and associations and in an etymological, social, and mythical history. Here the word becomes "encyclopaedic," open to the totality of associations that can be made with it. On the horizontal level, Trakl's poetry is ambiguous, capable of multiple, uncertain, and ever doubtful interpretations. It is the horizontal dimension, for example, to which Trakl's aura of rootedness in a mythical and Christian tradition must be connected. The "encyclopaedic" character of isolated words leads interpreters astray, but it has also produced such a wonderfully reflective essay as that of Heidegger on Trakl's words. Heidegger's thesis, however, is disputed by everyone, as well it might be, given the innumerable specifications that the word reduced to zero degree allows. By vertical I mean the purely personal and psychic dimension of language which is rooted in the closed recollections of the person, in the depths of his own personal and secret mythology and biology. Here the individual determines what a word refers to by his own private and closed use of the word. The private complex of associations that we have made with words and that we normally repress comes to the foreground. With the emergence of these private associational complexes, the conventional significance of words is entirely reordered.

On the vertical level Trakl's poetry is not ambiguous, but ambivalent, under the sway of contrary impulses. Because it is the vertical level which dominates in Trakl, traditional, classical criticism with its emphasis on the horizontal dimension misses most of what is the essence of Trakl. However, the attempts to track down Trakl's private use of words by compiling concordances and by using cross-reference approaches in order to delimit and to define the associational complexes surrounding his words and thereby also their meaning for him have not been successful. We find that there are no distinct associational complexes because they all intertwine with each other in one undefinable and unlimited complex. Thus where we hope to find a limit and a definition we find arbitrariness or a mass of material too large to be digested. We also find that the meaning of some of his most characteristic words is determinably ambivalent, that "silver," for example, can signify both guilt and guiltlessness, but that the ambivalence of other words exceeds pure opposition, for both antithetical meanings may be displaced in yet another context of merely contiguous and undefinable words. Still, if we assume then that the words in Trakl are largely arbitrary and that their significance is to be critically determined anew in each poem, we find that they are definitely bound, if not to an absolute meaning, at least to one modality of feeling or another in the poem; we feel, as Heidegger once put it, that "the ambiguity of this poetic speaking does not stream apart into an indeterminable ambiguity." But to be harried back and forth between a sense of meaninglessness and meaning, a sense that the words are absolutely arbitrary and fixed in an undefinable meaning, in an experience in madness.

One difference between Trakl and the Symbolists is that he did not arrive at his modernist poetic practice with its emphasis on the word by any conscious theory or method. He also did not court the experience of derangement as Rimbaud did; it overwhelmed him. In theory the Symbolists stressed the necessity of separating the expressive capacity of words from their abstract, creative capacity. They aspired to the "immaculate" or "pure" word which would be opaque, nontransparent, and purged of all the elements whose symbolic character leads us to the outside world of contexts. Their aim was to provoke the creativity inherent in language itself, the "mirage interne des mots mêmes" as Mallarmé put it. Naturally the creation of such a pure verbal poem is impossible. Words continue to be allied to meaning, and the liberation of the word, as Barthes points out, tends only to multiply these meanings. But the Symbolist attitude toward, and awe of, language is significant because it intuited the universe of the word as something transcending the rational, or functional, or relational. The Symbolist poets sensed that there is an impersonal and objective dimension in language itself or a creative mechanism within it which is beyond our conscious control. However, in Trakl the word is purged of conventional language and meaning in order to reveal not the abstract, creative power of the word but the unconscious and censored dimension of the individual. Also, his identification with the word did not allow him to experience the "liberation" of the word or a language dominated by unconscious processes as a positive condition.

His art is not, like Rimbaud's or Blake's, an attempt at mystical experience and visions of another outer dimension. Nor is it a mere experiment, a game with words, or an arbitrary, willful art of combinations. For Trakl the world of unconscious discourse with its mechanisms of condensation and displacement involved being in touch with what was the opposite of willful: the world of involuntary statements. The experience of an uncontrollable, arbitrary, and yet compulsive language must only have exacerbated his feeling of isolation and unreality—his sense of helplessness, impotence, and enervation and the feeling that he lacked control over himself and the world. Thus it seems difficult to speak of this phase as one of "visionary freedom." The poetry shows that he experienced his visionary existence as a painful kind of compulsion to reflect on himself and to order what seemed incapable of being ordered. What has often been called Trakl's narcissism is appallingly similar to the unloving self-scrutiny and the compulsive inspection of one's own mental and bodily processes that R. D. Laing describes as common in schizophrenia.

Trakl's own peculiar visionary style, very different from Rimbaud's, emerges, for example, in "Rest and Silence," written between March and September, 1913:

> Shepherds buried the sun in the bare forest.
> A fisherman hauled
> In a hair-spun net the moon from the freezing pond.
>
> In blue crystal
> Dwells the pale man, the cheek leaning on his stars;
> Or he bows his head in purple sleep.
>
> Yet ever touches the birds' black flight
> The visionary, the holiness of blue flowers,
> Thinks the near silence forgotten things, extinguished angels.
>
> Again the brow slumbers in lunar stones;
> A radiant youth
> Appears the sister in autumn and black corruption.

Even a casual reading of the poem makes evident that one must have a special experience with language here; one must forget that words are signs pointing to an exterior reality. From the latter perspective the poem plunges us into the mere semblance of a linguistic reality. The paucity of causal links, the interpenetration of images, and the metonymy have become extreme. Within the psychic time-space of the poem, all boundaries are effaced in a radical manner. Lines 8–9, the most complex lines of the poem, literally confuse the grammatical subject and predicate doubly or even triply. "The holiness of blue flowers" can be the grammatical predicate of "touches" together with "the birds' black flight," or it can conceivably be either the subject or predicate of the verb "thinks." But "thinks" may also belong to the subject "silence" or to the subject "the visionary." The paratactic ambiguity gives us a labyrinthine image of vision: the visionary sees the flowers seeing the silence's vision of "extinguished angels"; or, the visionary sees the flowers and the extinguished angels, which are remembered by "the near silence." Primary language is a language of desire and affects directed by interior unconscious processes. Thus, the shifting about of the sun and the moon signifies a change in the inner dimensions of the self; the closing of day and the advent of night are experienced as sacred happenings within the self. The cosmic imagery, which prepares for the vision proper and which suggests the psychic condensations and displacements that it entails, helps counteract the static, enervated, and immobile image of the mind that we are given. The uncanny power of the poem derives in part from the anonymity and indeterminateness of these processes of alteration in the psyche which the poem describes and from the juxtaposition of a sense of enervation with dynamic motion.

It is the strong visual impression that the poem makes which reminds one above all of Freud's description of dream formation. Here, as in the dream process, "thoughts are transformed into images, mainly visual. . . . verbal ideas are reduced to the corresponding things, on the whole as if the process were controlled by considerations of *suitability for plastic representation.*" The dream-work is not motivated by the coherence of verbal ideas; "it is always ready to exchange one word for another till it finds the expression most favorable for plastic representation." One is tempted to look at the words in the poem like objects in an abstract painting, luminous, evident, but obscure. The numerous words suggesting round objects (sun, moon, pond, crystal, head, stones) may then be seen as dispersed in a changing field of light. The color tones move from gold to gray to white in the first stanza, and in the second from blue to white to purple. In the second half of the poem we move further into the darker tones—to black—and then out again into the more neutral blue. We remain with the alternatives of black-white until the sister appears transformed to a youth, radiant in blackness. The epicene image of the sister connotes her identity with Trakl; and the temporal movement of the poem indicates that this indentity emerges from an indefinite past, forgotten, and frozen layer of experience. The color movement of the poem, which seems to seek a confrontation and fusion of opposite color values, recurs in the temporal movement. Temporality is apprehended largely spatially, as in primary temporal intuition, so that parts that exclude each other can be combined into a whole. In this manner precise and definite time distinctions and the notions of irreversibility, incompatibility, and irreparableness that accompany the pure temporal consciousness are avoided. The visionary excavation can recover what was light only in an imagined past-space.

Besides its intense visual and pictorial quality, the further reasons for speaking of the poetry of this phase as oneiric rather than schizophrenic are, first, that this poetry is, like the dream, narcissistic and concerned with the self, whereas in the final phase the cathexis with the self, or the concentration of emotional energy upon the self, is no longer evident. There is a cathexis only to words. Secondly, these poems, much more readily than the last ones, inspire interpretation, just as the dream does; the interpretations prove to be rather contradictory, because they all involve elaboration, addition, and the creation of missing connections by the interpreter, but even contradictory interpretations speak for an unconscious shaping will. Lastly, the emotional content of these poems does not exceed their pictorial objectification to the degree that it does in the later poems and in what Ludwig Binswanger calls the "dangerous dreams" of acute illness.

Just as Trakl's discontinuous images of his first phase originated partly from his discontinuous relationship to himself and the real world, so the oneiric and alienated language of this later phase suggests a secondary, more radical split within the true, melodic self. The identifiable, definable ego—the pronoun "I"—loses its primacy and disappears from his verse altogether in this phase. The "I" becomes volatilized, unreal, and more and more engaged in fantasized relationships with its own phantoms. It sinks back into the greater anonymity and flux of the more impersonal and unindividuated state where the ego can be another, or an object, or a series of others, and have many names, but not that of the simple, unifying "I." Thus, it is in this phase that Trakl creates his series of, one could almost say, epiclike poems about his newly divided and, hence, in a sense enlarged self: "Helian," "Elis," "Caspar Hauser Song," and "Sebastian in Dream." All these figures are projections of himself in a substitute, fantasy reality and passive purveyors of its visions. He also appears more and more frequently in such disembodied and effaced constructs as "ein Dunkles," meaning "a dark one" (an example of Trakl's own peculiar and untranslatable stylistic innovation where a neuter noun is formed from an adjective), or "ein Krankes" ("a sick one"), or "der Duldende" ("the patient one"), or "der Tönende" ("the sounding one"), or repeatedly as "ein Totes" ("a dead one"). The contemplation of all these imagined self-constructs creates a situation of discourse with aspects of oneself. The aim of the discourse is coherence: to gather together what Trakl experienced as insupportable in his experience, his dissociated self.

But for the visual-temporal structure that Trakl forged in his mature verse, his poems present us with a co-presence of things without fusion. The theme of self-reflection is distinguishable, but the reflection remains caught in itself and its self-fantasies, self-bounded, repetitious, vain, and incapable of delivering itself of its own magic circle of language. The effort to establish a coherent, continuous self is frustrated by interferences suggestive of internal conflicts that cannot be reached and, hence, cannot be solved. The relations between the split parts of the self become extremely complex and, in part, sadomasochistic; the questions of guilt or innocence—which self is guilty of what?—become paradoxical and unresolvable. The problematic, diseased emotional life ruptures the conjoining, healing efforts of fantasy. "Helian," for example, is extremely tautological both in its formal structure and in the numerous analogical figures that it creates. The figures move in a time-space that is both present and past, present and absent, imaginary and real. The time-space and the tautological nature of the poem remind us that we are in the unconscious where the mind is much more aware of the identity of things than of their difference. However, careful analysis of this, as of any Trakl poem, reveals a strong inner movement and countermovement, evident in the rhythm and syntactic structure, the constellation of colors and vocal sounds, and the change of tenses. But the significance of the movements—beyond the certainty that they portray an attempt at self-possession and an experience of ever-growing dispossession—is wholly open. Trakl fought disintegration by an abiding musical and painterly sense. Thus it becomes comprehensible why Trakl's variants are often determined by sound, by the desire to retain, for example, a certain sequence of vowels. A vowel sequence is a form of containment and order, a remnant, moreover, of his beautiful world of melos. Order, albeit one of abstract formal relationships, and sublanguage coherence seem in any event to be more primary than meaning when the issue at stake is loss of being.

A poem that is even more condensed and mystifying than "Rest and Silence," though written at about the same time or possibly earlier, is "Nightsong." It suggests why Trakl's futile self-reflection and rememoration could not be perpetuated and it seems to signal, the way a dream can, the augmentation of his disorder and disorientation. The poem dramatizes lived experience; there is a patent continuity between it and the letter quoted earlier in which Trakl spoke of "having died," and "trances to the point of stony torpidity." But it can only be interpreted if we try to imagine the alien and bizarre mental states that occur in an extreme schizoid condition.

> The breath of the Unmoved. An animal face
> Petrified before [with] the blue, of its holiness.
> Powerful is the silence in stone.
>
> The mask of a night bird. Soft triad
> Dies away in one. Elai! your countenance
> Bows itself speechlessly over bluish water.
>
> O! you silent mirrors of the truth.
> On the lonely one's ivory temples
> Appears the reflection of fallen angels.

The poem records an experience of alienation from human reflection. The effort at imaginary self-reflection and self-recognition produces a sense of reduction and loss. The very idea of reflection has potency; it overwhelms and shatters, and drives the self back into retreat rather than leading it forward to itself. Reflection impales and destroys reflection. The abyss between self-recognition as "animal face" and reflection as the nobler "countenance" is created by the self, but in it the poet is petrified. The experience objectifies the impotent subject in a language without dialectic. For when the power of language is reduced to the most fundamental antinomy of static and dynamic, dialectical reflection or discourse is cut off. And thus, a dialectical regression and progression of the kind that we normally associate with the achievement of art does not take place.

The ejection of words without a binding verb at the opening of each stanza, the iteration of words having to do with stone or petrification ("Unmoved," "petrified," "stone," "dies"), and the emphasis on "speechlessness" and, twice, on "silence" communicate a sense of arrestment, a fear of "stony torpidity." In opposition to these arrests there are words, fewer in number, suggesting animation and movement, but these are exactly the words that the poem undermines or cancels out by its activity of self-reflection. "Breath" suggests animation, but it is bound to "unmoved"; the equally paradoxical compound "animal face" petrifies, perhaps, into a "mask." Or, the more luminous image of the self as a singing "night bird" is a mere mask for the actual "animal face" of the self. The "triad" that suggests sound and movement "dies away." The recognition occurs "before" the blue breath of pure holiness in which the self does not participate. The self has only earthly reflections; in the "bluish" mirror of water only a narcissistic seeing of oneself is possible. Visually the poem moves into paleness or pallor, from "blue" to what is only "bluish," to the even paler "ivory" and the appearance of a reflection. The poem itself falls and dies away into what is already fallen. It comes to rest in a paradoxical image of suspended sinking motion, the "fallen angels." The inner sense of abandonment to sinking and falling is arrested only by the reflection that the fall has already occurred. In such an experience of retreat from an image of the self, the self becomes "speechless." There are no positive, progressive ways to project the self; self-visualization is frustrated.

Toward the latter half of this second phase Trakl's images break. The most basic metaphors of all, the bodily metaphors, are destroyed: eyes, mouth, head, arms, the human frame are shattered or broken. "Sink" comes to be the most common verb of his mature poetry and the transformation of images comes to be, as in "Nightsong," an experience of their sinking away: "O how everything sinks into the dark." The phenomenon of sinking into the semiconscious state of harmony, which was observable in the first phase, together with the phenomenon of reduction and loss, is now dominant. Light, sound, visions, and self-perceptions of the libido in the form of images are all increasingly reduced. He himself is now defined as "the sinking one." The reduction has as if to be reenacted or experienced repeatedly. The movement is always accompanied by sadness and melancholy, and thus it seems that this activity of mourning and melancholy has in fact to be repeated again and again. Accompanying the uncontrollable disappearance of all sounds and objects into darkness and silence is the lament of a loss of control over language. Trakl can no longer sing because his "mouth" is "broken"—because "A purple flame/ Fails in my mouth. In the silence/ Dies the frightened soul's lonely lyre music." The melancholy singing turns to speechless staring. Already in 1912, Trakl had said to Karl Röck, his friend and later editor: "One cannot express oneself in poetry. One cannot express oneself at all." The statement epitomizes the dilemma of his life. Now "unspeakable" begins to be a recurrent word both in his letters and in his poetry: "Unspeakable is all that, O God, so that one breaks shaken unto one's knees," "The night and speechless a forgotten life." "O despair that breaks unto its knees with a dumb cry."

Before boarding the train in 1914 to take part in World War I, Trakl handed a brief note to Ficker containing these words:

Feeling in the moments of deathlike existence: All human beings are worthy of love. Awaking you feel the world's bitterness; therein lies all your unresolved guilt; your poem an imperfect atonement.

It is the only statement that we have from Trakl about his art after the first phase, no doubt because such a statement would suggest a self-consciousness and a sense of distance and of goal that he could no longer possess or achieve. The note points—as does so much else—to a split form of existence: a conscious state of bitterness and guilt and a dreamlike, deathlike state of positive feelings toward mankind. The poem only mediates between them imperfectly: it cannot reconcile the two states. The note also makes evident what comes to be a tremendous ethical obsession in the latter part of Trakl's second phase, an attempt to resolve his ambivalence in ethical and religious categories. His one remaining wish, as he put it in a letter of January, 1914, was "to be purified or destroyed." Poetry, so Trakl had always seemingly felt, was a secondary activity, an atonement for failure in what was primary. For him, not art but the need for love was supreme. "All poetry-making is nothing," he said to Karl Röck in 1912; "what need has one for poems and the World as Will and Idea, when one has the Evangel. A few words of the Evangel have more life and world and knowledge of men than all these poems: 'Blessed are the poor in spirit for theirs is the Kingdom of Heaven.' Next to this poets are so dispensable, so stupid." One cannot, indeed, atone for an ethical guilt with an aesthetic work, but the comparison and the devaluation of poetry are, nonetheless, odd. Still, they point to Trakl's need for release precisely through a symbol — through the authentically symbolic words that he could never find — which would magically heal his "broken world" in language. "It is unique," he said in a conversation with Carl Dallago, "how Christ solves the deepest problems of mankind with each simple word."

Trakl's attempts to create a benign substitute reality fail. As at the end of the first phase, his anxiety returns, now, in the form of dread and self-reproaches. The antitheses and ambivalence intensify. The sharpening of antitheses into a rigid either-or stance is, for Binswanger, *the* ontological structure of schizophrenic existence, which can finally only end in "a renunciation of the whole antinomic problem." Ambivalence, the fact that every tendency is balanced by a contrary one, is normal; the manifest struggle between opposites that we see in Trakl is not. He is in the grip of a compulsion to produce contrary associations — a phenomenon that E. Bleuler called "negative suggestibility" — where the control of the psyche is too weak to promote or inhibit either the positive or negative approach. Trakl becomes the victim of an uncontrolled counterplay of positive and negative. At the beginning of this phase Trakl's efforts seem to have been directed more often at pushing the positive associations. His attempt to idealize his relationship to his sister and to create a "blue paradise" of childhood innocence testifies to this. Helian, Caspar Hauser, Elis, and Sebastian are figures who are innocent or innocently guilty. Similarly, the dead or unborn youth whom Trakl encounters repeatedly in his poems is innocent and guiltless. His identification with the Christ figure, the archetypal image of the higher, ideal self, also confirms this, though his introjection of the Christ figure also rests upon an identification with solitude, isolation, suffering, the notion of an early death, and the sense of not being understood. The really pathological element in this identification becomes evident in a reported conversation between Trakl and Dallago, in which Trakl said, "I am Christ," and in his often cited reaction to a mounted calf's head at a village festival; on seeing the head Trakl trembled visibly and said, "This is our Lord Christ."

Trakl's prose poems "The Transformation of Evil," "Dream and Benightedness," and "Revelation and Decline" are attempts to escape the intolerably exacerbated ambivalence by stressing the negative associations. In these poems Trakl presents himself relentlessly as guilty. They are a complete and stark autobiography of the nightmarish visions and hallucinations in which he lived. They are an account of the "black hell of his heart," "the stony hell" in which his "countenance died." The roots of the despair and condemnation are in the family:

As silent ones they gathered at the table; as dying ones they broke with waxen hands the bleeding bread. Woe to the stony eyes of the sister as at supper her madness passed to the nocturnal forehead of the brother, as the bread turned to stone under the suffering hands of the mother. O the decayed ones, as they with silver tongues kept silent the hell.

Dreaming and petrification, fantasy and affects contend in the prose poems. "But as I climbed down the rocky path, madness seized me, and I screamed loud into the night; and as I bowed with silver fingers over the silent water, I saw that my countenance had left me. And the white voice spoke to me: Kill yourself!" He lives tormented in a living death, for a part of him has died, but other aspects of the self and the affects continue to live to tear him apart and to restore him. "And ever darker melancholy clouds the departed head, horrible lightning frightens the nocturnal soul, your hands tear apart my breathless breast. . . . and as I died looking on, fear and deepest pain die in me; and the blue shadow of the youth raises itself radiant in the dark, gentle song; on lunar wings over the greening tips, the crystal cliffs, rises the white countenance of the sister." But in the next transformation the positive image is destroyed: "I concealed the head silently in purple linen; and the earth threw out a child-like corpse, a lunar shape, which stepped slowly out of my shadow, sank down a stony cataract with broken arms, flocculent snow." The attempt to halt the deranged ambivalence even if through a negation of the self still suggests a will for a resolution. But the simultaneous presence of, and submission to, "sinking" also suggests that the ambivalence is not opposed and hence that his dissociation can no longer be halted.

The ethical self-condemnation that comes to predominate in the prose poems and which may have been Trakl's way to arrest his ambivalence in a negative manner is also echoed in a letter to Ficker in June, 1913:

> Too little love, too little justice and pity, and ever too little love; all too much hardness, pride and all kinds of felony—that is I. I am certain that I leave off the bad only out of weakness and cowardice and thereby furthermore shame my badness. I long for the day on which the soul can and will no longer want to live in this unhappy, with melancholy polluted body, on which she will leave this ridiculous form of filth and decay, which is only an all too true mirror image of a godless, accursed century.
>
> God, only a small spark of pure joy—and one would be saved; love—and one would be redeemed.

In the letter Trakl is not only asking for love, but accusing himself of lovelessness and doubting his own capacity to love. Still, in the self-accusation there is an element of pride; he feels himself to be representative. A few months later even this small spark of self-worth is gone; he is "small and unhappy." By November, 1913, Trakl's crises and depressions seem to have come to a climax. He writes to Ficker, in a much quoted letter, that his world has broken apart:

> In recent days such terrible things have happened to me, that I can never rid myself of their shadow my life long. Yes . . . my life has been unspeakably broken apart in the last few days and only a wordless pain remains to which even any bitterness is denied. . . .
> I no longer know my way in or out. It is a so nameless unhappiness when the world breaks in two for one. O my God, what a judgment has broken in over me. Tell me that I must still have the strength to live and to do what is the true. Tell me that I am not insane. A stony darkness has broken in. O my friend, how small and unhappy I have become.

We are not certain what the "terrible things" to which Trakl refers are. Ficker connected them to Trakl's worries about his sister, whose marriage was in difficulties. In any case, in March, 1914, after she had a nearly fatal miscarriage, Trakl rushed to Berlin, and returned looking absolutely destroyed. At this time he painted a rather frightening self-portrait which represents him as he had appeared to himself in a mirror one night. One friend described it as "a mask." Otto Basil, Trakl's biographer, writes: "Eyes, nose and mouth are dark caves, the face is as if decayed, largely blue-green, with purple spots on the cheeks. The mouth is torn open as if crying noiselessly." At approximately the same time Trakl wrote a "Dramafragment," which exposes his fatal love-hate relationship to his sister, and in December, 1913, and March, 1914, three truly ecstatic poems, "Western Song," "Soul's Springtime," and "Song of the Departed." The coming into being, particularly, of the poems, in the midst of an acute state of depression, has puzzled some critics. But a manic reaction or a sudden feeling of self-sufficiency and potency under renewed pressure from reality—and that the Grete episode obviously was—is not uncommon in a schizoid condition where the relationship between the different, split selves is fundamentally ambivalent or persecutory.

"Western Song" begins with the ecstatic cry: "O the soul's nocturnal wingbeat" and ends with the famous lines:

> But radiant the lovers raise the silver eyelids:
> One sex. Incense pours from rosy pillows
> And the sweet song of the resurrected.

"Soul's Springtime," beginning "Outcry in sleep," celebrates a momentary sense of attained purity and peace:

> Purity! Purity! Where are the terrible pathways of death,
> Of gray stony silence, the cliffs of night
> And the peaceless shadows? Radiant abyss of sunlight.

"O life in the ensouled blue of the night," Trakl exclaims in the more subdued, but peaceful "Song of the Departed":

> For more radiant ever awakens out of black minutes of
>   insanity
> The patient one on a stony threshold
> And he is powerfully embraced by the cool blue and the
>   shining decline of autumn.

With Freud, who sees the manic phase in melancholia in the light of a regression to a primal narcissism and all that becomes available to the ego as a result of it, we can say that the poems celebrate the fulfillment of Trakl's deepest wish fantasies. The further withdrawal of libido into the self in reaction to the traumatic experience with Grete stirred these fantasies from his depths and made possible the momentary, blissful experience of the absolute union of primordial opposites. The fantasy is necessary because Trakl had already, in a sense, lost his sister three times, once through the incest taboo, again because of her infidelities to him, and then with her marriage. The most recent event threatened a final loss. The loss of a love object chosen originally on a narcissistic basis can, according to Freud, be counteracted by a regression of the object-cathexis into narcissism. A part of the ego is altered by identification with the beloved object and therefore the love relationship need not be given up. That Grete became a clear and dominant image in Trakl's poetry exactly at the time of her marriage in July, 1912, tends to confirm that he incorporated her as his word, as his "dark melody," in a more intense and spiritualized relationship. She is connected to his mouth: "Silently lives/ On your mouth the autumnal moon/ Drunk with the poppies' dark song." Now, in the ecstasy of these poems he reasserts his possession and control over this word and momentarily the sense of inner union is complete.

His sister's crisis is the only possible external event which could have shaken Trakl severely. But the "terrible things" that his letter to Ficker speaks about were probably internal: an increase of his experiences of terror and paralysis, and the completion of that inner fragmentation which his poems announce. The desirable fantasy world, fractured by deeper complexes, comes to an end. The subsequent internal catastrophe appears in the projections of the end of the world of his final poems. Even if reason could be given for characterizing Trakl's condition up to this point as a neurosis or even as a severe schizoid condition, there is little doubt that he is now in the grip of a psychosis. Perhaps Trakl's inner tensions and ambivalence reached a point where they were simply no longer tolerable to him. Schizophrenia is a condition, one can then speculate, that offered Trakl a way out of the sterile and unending struggle of reaction-formations by eliminating the possibility of repression altogether. In schizophrenia the possibility of repression as such is thwarted because consciousness and the unconscious coalesce. Schizophrenic language, therefore, according to Freud, is not built on repression, as all normal language is, but is dependent on negation and rejection. That which is expulsed or negated cannot return from the unconscious, as the repressed does, because it is simply abolished from the realm of the possible. Hence the repressed can only reappear as if from without in the form of a hallucination. The subject cannot see the inner origin of the hallucination because he has lost the ability to distinguish between inner and outer on all levels. It is characteristic that the appearance of the hallucination leaves the subject speechless.

If the unbearable visions at the end of the second phase indicate a return of the repressed in a violent and dreadful form, with personal visions of punishment, murder predominating, then Trakl's terse, impersonal, and prophetic poems of 1914, with their visions of cosmic disaster, indicate the return of an expulsion from without in the form of visionary hallucinations. These lines from "Occident" and "Limbo," for example, were written before the war, in March and April, 1914, respectively:

> Powerfully breeding fear
> In the thunderclouds
> The spasmodic evening red.
> You dying peoples!
> Pale surge
> Breaking on the beach of night,
> Falling stars.
>
> And from blackish gates
> Angels step forth with cold foreheads;
> Blue, the death-laments of mothers.
> There rolls through her long hair
> A fiery wheel, the round day
> Of earth's torture without end.

The imagery of these poems on the whole corresponds closely to Jung's description of the primary symptoms in schizophrenia: "It is as if the very foundations of the psyche were giving way, as if an explosion or an earthquake were tearing asunder the structure of a normally built house. . . . They [the symptoms] appear in projection as earthquakes, cosmic catastrophes, the fall of the stars, the splitting of the sun, the falling asunder of the moon, the transformation of people into corpses, the freezing of the universe, and so on." It is the return of the expulsed powerfully from without that gives these poems their character of having won back a sense of reality, as most critics put it. But the sense of reality is there, not because Trakl reestablished a contact with the concrete things represented by words, but rather because he lost this contact utterly. His disease gives his language the status of the real. The experience of schizophrenia is most likely the tragic, psychic history behind what has often been called, not inaccurately but on other grounds, Trakl's unconscious signaling of the reality of the Great War in his last poems.

What distinguishes the handful of poems of Trakl's final phase in 1914 from the poems of the second phase is that in them we confront what may be called schizophrenic language rather than dream language. The transference to language has now become an absolute and exclusive identification with words alone. Trakl's final substitution and reconstruction is the world and the self as the word. The word becomes in him—to borrow from Jacques Lacan—"the Real object" which "swallows up the functions of language." The word dominates; it has wholly lost its mediating function and significance, and is an end in itself. Trakl's last style is a nominal style. Language is reduced primarily to nouns, which are closer to the roots of words and of language as such. On the one hand, the simplification reduces the possibility of ambivalence, the necessity and dread of word choices and sentence elaboration through verbs, adjectives, and so on. On the other hand, single words now stand for what were formerly entire images, or whole sentences, or possibly even poems. The word-condensation is extreme. The radically truncated style leaves no room for the earlier long, elegiac lines, or for the work of dream-formation: for the creation of strange time-spaces, the transformation of words into preverbal visual images, the theatrical staging of the self in various situations, or the self-perceptions of the libido in visions. The elaborate and arduous work of the dream is eliminated. All elaboration is abolished. Grammar and syntax, which came under the control of the primary process of condensation and displacement in the second phase, are also reduced. Now words alone are under the control of the primary process. Trakl's last cathexis is to words. But by this final maneuver of reduction Trakl also possesses his world as never before. All obstruction is eliminated; the word is instinct and energy, essence and authority; it can exclaim, lament, or condemn in a demonic and prophetic way in its uninhibited power.

> Powerful you are dark mouth
> In the interior, shape
> Formed of autumn clouds,
> Golden evening stillness;
> A greenly darkening mountain torrent
> In broken Scotch pines
> Shadow-district;
> A village
> That dies devout in brown images.

The extreme condensation and abbreviation that characterizes Trakl's last poems makes these lines from "Melancholy" a nearly unintelligible structure of word constellations. The dominating instinct behind the words seems to be that of expulsion, the original form of negation. The impulse of introduction into the ego has failed; the fundamental instincts of affirmation and negation are defused, and in a verse that appears to be commanded by an instinct to disavow and to discharge, we witness a destruction of cosmic proportions.

Trakl's very last projection is that of his own end. In the poem "Lament" the animosity against the self or the world, evident earlier, is absent. The persecutory passions are spent. The letters from the mental hospital in Cracow, where the poem was written, give us a glimpse of his state of mind. He speaks of "falling into an unspeakable melancholy," and after Ficker's visit to him there he writes that he is "doubly sad." The melancholy that seems simply to have overwhelmed him is a condition from which he was never free and the melancholy tone which characterizes all of his poems attests to this. But "Lament" is beyond melancholy. Freud's description of melancholia as a disease of the superego where "dissatisfaction with the self on moral grounds is far the most outstanding feature" illuminates aspects of Trakl's earlier self-condemnations and his ethical concern, but not the resistless self-surrender enacted in this poem. Here some last remnant of the self simply watches the most vital part of the self—the voice—succumb to extinction. The sense conveyed is not that of self-condemnation but that of self-negation and exhaustion.

In "Lament" the sister also appears, but it is fearful to see that she appears only as the higher goddess, the supreme being. She is the persisting conscience, the "sister of stormy melancholy," called upon to see the final shipwreck of the ego. She is that part of Trakl that once truly ardently loved and that sought to escape annihilation in him by retreating into his ego. She is the word, the creation of word-relationships, Trakl's innermost, vital self, and his last way of loving and being connected. Now that loving word-conscience is called up to witness its own demise.

> Sleep and death, the somber eagles
> Resound nightlong around this head:
> Would [might] the icy wave
> Of eternity swallow
> Man's golden image. On horrible reefs
> The purple body is shattered.
> And the dark voice laments
> Over the sea.

> Sister of stormy melancholy
> See, a fearful boat sinks down
> Under stars,
> From the silent face of night.

Trakl sees his existence in the image of the sinking "boat." He is "fearful" because the only two final alternatives are "sleep and death." Sleep is the involuntary, passive sinking into extinction as into the inevitable, and even, the desirable. Death is the violent experience of destruction that makes itself felt in the "shattered" body. It is the remnant of a consciousness of death as change and as the other, "the icy wave." The dark lamenting "voice" takes note of a final ambivalence: "verschlänge" means both "would swallow" and "might swallow" in German. Is death wished for or feared? But there is a further ambivalence. The death instinct itself has split apart. Destruction is only *one* form in which the death instinct exhibits itself. In its other form, the death instinct is that which is mute; the desire for death does not speak; it is the loss of the desire to speak. "The silent face of night" is the universe before we have acquired language. It is also the death instinct in the form of muteness. Silence is Thanatos, language is Eros. The erotic expressive part of the self watches another part of itself succumb to speechlessness. The poem balances on the edges of the primal repression, that of the death instinct. The repression exhibits itself as a last agon between expression and silence. At the conclusion, the primal repression is thwarted. The silence that Trakl had always fought and feared, and loved, that was present in his poetry in its pauses, now becomes supreme. The inexpressible overwhelms him. Since we know that in schizophrenia suicide is always possible and unpredictable, and that in this condition all repression is thwarted in a coalescence of the unconscious and consciousness, we can also say that in this condition the most primal repression of all is in danger of being lifted at any moment, and that *this* is what the poem expresses.

Both dream language and schizophrenic language are determined by the unconscious, by the primary mental process. For Freud, as far as language is concerned, the difference between a conscious and an unconscious idea is that the former "comprises the concrete idea plus the verbal idea corresponding to it" and the latter comprises that "of the thing alone." It follows that a language dominated by the unconscious should always be a thing-language, and this is indeed true of dreams. The extraordinary phenomenon of schizophrenia in respect to language, as Freud brilliantly realized, is that here "*words* are subject to the same process as that which makes dream-images out of dream-thoughts. . . . They undergo condensation, and by means of displacement transfer their cathexis to one another without remainder; the process may extend so far that a single word, which on account of its manifold relations is especially suitable, can come to represent a whole train of thought." But a poem that is a dream composed of words—where words are subject to the activities of the primary process—is one that we cannot possibly hope to understand. The final Trakl poem is like a set of words caught in a space of mirrors. In the poems the word is cut off both from the images that the unconscious could bring it and from the concrete idea that consciousness could contribute. It is a language excommunicated from the interior and the exterior world; it designates nothing in any direction. But it is powerfully dynamic and dramatic, nonetheless, because it is naked primary process.

When we read such forceful and beautiful lines as these in the late Trakl: "O heart/ Glistening over into snowy coolness," we can make guesses about what the words separately and in conjunction might mean, but finally the lines are hermetic. The aesthetic quality of such lines, however, declares that the aesthetic sense is anterior to any processes or changes that the human psyche may endure. It can attach itself to the primary process and influence its activities of displacement and condensation. The deranged mind cannot create the intelligible symbolic discourse that is the privilege of the authentic indissoluable imagination, but it can without cessation strive to fasten the awfulness of derangement in formal patterns. It would seem important to accept and understand the mute radiance of Trakl's art not despite his disease, or by repressing the fact of his disease, but only together with it because we will better understand the art that we have always valued when we bring an art carved purely out of the unconscious into our total perspective of what art is.

SELECTED BIBLIOGRAPHY

Principal Works of Georg Trakl in German

Dichtungen und Briefe. Ed. Walther Killy and Hans Szklenar. 2 vols. Salzburg, Otto Müller, 1969.

Principal Works of Georg Trakl in English

Twenty Poems of Georg Trakl. Tr. James Wright and Robert Bly. Madison, Minn., The Sixties Press, 1961.

Selected Poems. Ed. Christopher Middleton and tr. Robert Grenier, Michael Hamburger, David Luke, and C. Middleton. London, Cape, 1968.

Georg Trakl Poems. Tr. Lucia Getsi. Athens, Ohio, Mundus Artium Press, 1973.

Critical Works and Commentary

Basil, Otto. Georg Trakl in Selbstzeugnissen und Bilddokumenten. Hamburg, Rowohlt, 1965.

Blass, Regine. Die Dichtung Georg Trakls: Von der Trivialsprache zum Kunstwerk. Berlin, Erich Schmidt, 1968.

Brinkmann, Richard. Expressionismus: Forschungsprobleme 1952–1960, pp. 30–42, 83–87. Stuttgart, Metzler, 1961.

Casey, T. J. Manshape that Schone: An Interpretation of Trakl. Oxford, Blackwell, 1964.

Dietz, Ludwig. Die lyrische Form Georg Trakls. Trakl-Studien V. Salzburg, Otto Müller, 1959.

Erinnerung an Georg Trakl. Innsbruck, Brenner, 1926.

Falk, Walter, Leid und Verwandlung: Rilke, Kafka, Trakl und der Epochenstil des Impressionismus und Expressionismus. Trakl-Studien VI. Salzburg, Otto Müller, 1961.

Focke, Alfred. Georg Trakl: Liebe und Tod. Vienna, Herold, 1955.

George, Emery E. "On Seeing and Hearing the Poem: An Experiment with Trakl's 'Afra,'" *Orbis Litterarum*, XXI (1966), 202–21.

Goldmann, Heinrich. Katabasis: Eine tiefenpsychologische Studie zur Symbolik der Dichtung Georg Trakls. Trakl-Studien IV. Salzburg, Otto Müller, 1957.

Grimm, Reinhold. "Georg Trakls Verhältnis zu Rimbaud," *Germanisch-Romanische Monatsschrift*, N.S. IX (1959), 288–315.

Hamburger, Michael. Contraries: Studies in German Literature, pp. 291-323. New York, E. P. Dutton & Co., Inc., 1970.
Heidegger, Martin. "Georg Trakl: Eine Erörterung seines Gedichtes," *Merkur*, VII (1953), 226-58.
Hermand, Jost. "Der Knabe Elis: Zum Problem der Existenzstufen bei Georg Trakl," *Monatshefte*, LI (1959), 225-36.
Heselhaus, Clemens. "Die Elis-Gedichte von Georg Trakl," *Deutsche Vierteljahrsschrift*, XXVIII (1954), 384-413.
——Deutsche Lyrik der Moderne von Nietzsche bis Yvan Goll, pp. 228-57. Düsseldorf, A. Bagel, 1962.
Höllerer, Walter. "Trübsinn" and "Grodek," in Die deutsche Lyrik: Form und Geschichte, ed. Benno von Wiese, II, 409-24. Düsseldorf, A. Bagel, 1957.
Killy, Walther. Über Georg Trakl. Göttingen, Vandenhoek und Ruprecht, 1960.
Lachmann, Eduard. Kreuz und Abend: Eine Interpretation der Dichtungen Georg Trakls. Trakl-Studien I. Salzburg, Otto Müller, 1954.
Lindenberger, Herbert. Georg Trakl. New York, Twayne Publishers, 1971.
Neumann, Erich. Der schöpferische Mensch, pp. 247-310. Zurich, Rhein, 1959.
Prawer, Siegbert. "Grammatical Reflections on Trakl's 'De Profundis,'" *German Life and Letters*, N.S. XXII (1968), 48-59.
Preisendanz, Wolfgang. "Auflosung und Verdinglichung in den Gedichten Georg Trakls," in Immanente Ästhetik/Ästhetische Reflexion, ed. W. Iser, pp 227-61, 485-94. Munich, Fink, 1966.
Rey, W. H. "Heidegger-Trakl: Einstimmiges Zwiegespräch," *Deutsche Vierteljahrsschrift*, XXX (1956), 89-136.
Ritzer, Walter. Trakl-Bibliographie. Trakl-Studien III. Salzburg, Otto Müller, 1956.
Schneider, Karl Ludwig. Der bildhafte Ausdruck in den Dichtungen Georg Heyms, Georg Trakls und Ernst Stadlers: Studien zum lyrischen Sprachstil des deutschen Expressionismus. Heidelberg, Winter, 1954.
Simon, Klaus. Traum und Orpheus: Eine Studie zu Georg Trakls Dichtungen. Trakl-Studien II. Salzburg, Otto Müller, 1955.
Sokel, Walter. The Writer in Extremis: Expressionism in Twentieth-Century German Literature, pp. 49-50, 72-78. Stanford, Stanford University Press, 1959.
Spoerri, Theodor. Georg Trakl: Strukturen in Persönlichkeit und Werk. Bern, Francke, 1954.

Staiger, Emil. "Zu einem Gedicht Georg Trakls," *Euphorion,* LX (1961), 279–96.

Szklenar, Hans. "Beiträge zur Chronologie und Anordnung von Georg Trakls Gedichten auf Grund des Nachlasses von Karl Röck," *Euphorion,* LX (1966), 222–62.

Times Literary Supplement (9.7.70), p. 752.

Walter, Jürgen. "Orientierung auf der formalen Ebene—Paul Klee und Georg Trakl: Versuch einer Analogie," *Deutsche Vierteljahrsschrift,* XLII (1968), 637–61.

Wetzel, Heinz. Klang und Bild in den Dichtungen Georg Trakls. Göttingen, Vandenhoek und Ruprecht, 1968.

Wölfel, Kurt. "Entwicklungsstufen im lyrischen Werk Georg Trakls," *Euphorion,* LII (1958), 50–81.